Economics, Business and Artificial Intelligence Common Knowledge Terms And Definitions

STEVE DAFOE

Economics, Business and Artificial Intelligence Common Knowledge Terms And Definitions

Print Book ISBN 978-1-304-63479-5

Table of Contents

INTRODUCTION

Recently, I have been learning about General Artificial Intelligence and the implications it will have in our lives. The array of opinions crosses the full spectrum from the wonderful ways it will improve our lives to the fear it could unleash a 'Self-Controlled Superintelligence' that may not align itself with human social and ethical constructs. This subject is a fast-moving rocket, and it is important that everyone understands some key terms when it comes to Artificial Intelligence. Whether you know it or not, AI touches your lives today and in future, will increase exponentially as it exerts this massive influence on each one of us.

Being a student of Economics and Business, I always seek to refresh my knowledge of key common terms in these areas. Economics, Business and Politics overlap a great deal in both academic and real-world applications. Artificial Intelligence will hopefully add for the better, the fields of Business, Politics and Economics. AI has the potential to revolutionize the way business operates and contribute to global economic activity. Everything from sales and marketing, customer service and operations will benefit as the data mined by AI will allow for better decision-making and optimization of business operations.

Contained within is a small list of common terms in the areas of Economics, Business and Artificial Intelligence. Political terms are not included here but you will read some definitions of Economics that do have an overlap of political inferences.

I hope these terms and definitions provide some insight into the world of economics, business, and artificial intelligence. These all affect your life more than you realize.

CHAPTER 1

ECONOMIC Terms A—D

Acid Test Ratio

The Acid test compares a company's position with short term assets to short term liabilities to see if there is enough cash to pay immediate debt problems. Ideally a ratio of 1 or greater indicates a firm's ability to pay. Can also be applied to Individuals as a litmus test of one's ability to pay short term debt at any given time.

Absolute Advantage

A concept of international trade. If country A is better at making cars than country B, and B is better at making furniture than A, it makes sense for each country to focus on the area where they have this advantage, and then trade cars for furniture. Usually, an abundance of raw materials helps countries attain this type of advantage for what they can produce most profitably.

Active management

A form of Investing that attempts to outperform other investors, (such as Investment Managers operating large ETF's or Mutual Funds) by selecting a limited number of assets and trading them regularly. As opposed to Passive Mgt like investing in an Index fund where stocks and investments are predetermined already, and change is not a predominant feature.

Adverse selection

A risk associated with most types of insurance. People who are worried about their health will be more inclined to pay for health or Life insurance than those who are very fit. Often with higher premiums. One way to avoid the problem is to make insurance compulsory for all, as happens with Group Benefits Plans. This is spread the risk over a larger pool of people.

Agency costs

The expense involved in using a third party to carry out a task. Examples include hiring a fund manager to look after an investment portfolio, or the cost to Taxpayers of having a Nursing agency provide Nurses directly to Health care facilities in Canada.

Aggregate demand

This is a macroeconomic term that measures the total amount of demand for all finished products and services in an economy. The four components that determine this are Consumer spending, Investment spending, Government spending and Net exports. Demand can fall, even if people's income and wealth are unchanged or even increase, if they decide to save, rather than spend.

Alpha

That part of an investment return that is due to the skill of the fund manager. This can be very hard to measure. Note to achieve this, see above on '"Active Management".

Amortisation

The gradual reduction in the value of an asset (or a debt) over time. A debt (such as a mortgage) is amortised via regular repayments. Companies use amortisation to steadily reduce the value of Intangible assets on their balance-sheets.

Appreciation

The rise in the value of an asset. Your Home is often described as appreciating when the value of real estate rises. Conversely, depreciation is a fall of an asset over time.

Asset

Something that can be used to create economic value. Your home, your investments, or your car. An asset can be tangible, such as a business building and machinery or it can be intangible, such as a patent, goodwill, or a brand name. Assets make up one side of a company's balance-sheet; the other is liabilities.

Asset stripping

The practice of buying a company and rapidly selling off the component parts with the aim of making a profit. This often leads to great disruption in the business and a loss of jobs.

Asset value

One measure used by investors to calculate the worth of a company. Normally, a company's debts are deducted to calculate a net asset value. The same measure can be applied to an individual and family to help determine personal financial health.

Auctions

Usually associated with estate sales, livestock, antiques, and works of art. But in recent decades, they have been favoured by economists as a means of ensuring that sellers get the best price for a wider range of assets.

Authoritarian capitalism

Usually applied to Communist or Socialist countries such as China and Russia. This describes economies in which big business co-exists with an authoritarian government. Businesses are allowed to make money but if they dare to criticize the government, or appear too independent, they may face criminal or financial sanctions. Also, it usually supports Oligarchy in Russia where politicians and businessmen are a small but all-inclusive power structure onto themselves that benefits by oppression and public obedience.

Balance of payments

A term used to describe a country's transactions with the rest of the world. The import and export of goods and services are captured in the Current Account, which also includes investment income and transfers. The Capital Account reflects financial transactions such as Foreign Direct Innvestment or purchases of equities and bonds. These will balance in the sense that a current-account deficit (or surplus) must be offset by a capital-account surplus (or deficit).

Balance-sheet

In accounting, a statement of the assets and liabilities of a business. It must balance in the sense that assets equal liabilities. The assets such as cash or equipment or inventory are being used in the business; the liabilities show how those assets were funded whether in the form of debt (owed to creditors) or equity (owed to owners or shareholders).

Bank rate

Term used in Canada and the USA to describe the official rate set by the Central Bank like the Federal Reserve or Bank of Canada when it pays interest to commercial banks. By manipulating this rate, the Central Bank affects the level of rates that businesses and consumers pay to borrow money.

Bank run.

In a crisis, bank depositors may start to doubt they will get their money back. So, they may demand to withdraw it. Since banks have lent out this money, it is impossible for them to repay all depositors instantly. The bank may fail. To avoid this, most countries have schemes of Deposit Insurance. In Canada there is CDIC that protects individuals to set amounts depending on the type of Savings involved.

Barter

The direct swap of goods and services for other goods and services, without the use of money. This is normally a less efficient form of trade since the wants and needs of buyers and sellers rarely match exactly.

Basis point

One hundredth of a percentage point. The term is often used to describe interest rate changes. A quarter-percentage-point rise or fall in rates is described as 25 basis points.

Bear Outlook

Investor who expects the price of an asset or assets in general to fall. A Bear Market is usually a fall of 20% in a stock market like the Dow Jones.

Behavioural economics

School of thought that believes that the economic decisions of individuals are often driven by psychological biases rather than the rational analysis of expected returns. One example is the Endowment Effect. Individuals value the goods they own more highly than they would pay for the same item in an open market.

Beta

This ratio measures the sensitivity of an asset's price to that of the overall market. A stock that tends to go up even more rapidly than the market when it is rising, and drop more precipitously when it is falling, is described as "high beta"; one that moves less violently than the market is "low beta".

Bill of exchange

A short-term financial instrument, originally used to finance international trade. The buyer of goods would give the seller a signed bill, equal to the value of the purchase, which the seller could then cash with a banker. In modern finance, bills are a catch-all term for short-term debt such as US Treasury Bills and commercial bills.

Blockchain

A distributed ledger used to make a digital record of the ownership of cryptocurrencies.

Bonds

IOUs issued by a borrower which normally promise repayment of the money on a set date (the maturity) with regular interest payments during the life of the bond. The riskier the issue, the higher the interest rate (or yield) on the bond. Governments issue bonds to cover the gap between the amount they receive in taxes and the amount they spend. Companies issue bonds to finance investment programmes.

Bretton Woods Agreement

A significant point in Economic history. Located in New Hampshire this community hosted a conference in 1944 which mapped the post-war economic order. This is the birthplace of the IMF

(International Monetary Fund) and the World Bank. In addition, it created a system that linked all currencies at fixed exchange rates to the dollar, which was convertible into gold at a set price.

Bubble

The concept that asset prices can rise far higher than can be justified by their fundamentals, such as the expected cashflows that will derive from them.

Budget

The annual process through which a government sets out its spending plans and tax measures. A balanced budget is when revenues are expected to match expenditure. More usually, spending outstrips revenues, and the government runs a budget deficit. Creating or expanding a deficit can be a deliberate act to boost an economy. A key feature of Keynesian Economics.

Bull

Investor who expects the price of an asset or assets in general to rise.

Business cluster

When companies in an industrial sector gather in a specific area, such as Automobile manufacturing in Detroit or technology companies in Silicon Valley. When a cluster forms, companies will find it easier to attract high-skilled staff, workers have a wider choice of employers, innovations can circulate more quickly, and start-up companies may find it easier to get finance.

Business cycle

Another term to describe the way that economies tend to expand and contract over time. Various economists have tried to calculate the length of a typical cycle, but these have varied widely over history. Booms tend to be much longer than busts, particularly in recent times.

Bust

A sudden economic contraction, also known as a recession. (which is defined as a period of temporary economic decline during which trade and industrial activity are reduced, generally identified by a fall in GDP in two successive quarters)

Capital

A word that serves a lot of purposes in economics. It is used to refer to the investment that an individual businessperson puts into a new business (hence Capitalism); to any lump sum of money or financial resources that has been saved; and more broadly to the people and institutions who invest in the world's financial marketplace. It is also synonymous with a bank's equity capital.

Capital account

In international trade, the component of the balance of payments that comprises financial transactions, such as foreign direct investment. On a company's balance-sheet, the capital account largely comprises the equity capital invested by the owners and retained profits.

Capital asset pricing model

A financial model that relates the return of an asset class to its riskiness. It is based on the idea of a risk-free asset , usually defined as Federal government bonds. Investors in riskier assets (like equities) should demand a higher return than they get from government bonds to reflect the greater risk of loss. This risk relates to the beta of the asset concerned.

Capital flight

What happens when investors try to avoid high taxes, or the prospect of currency devaluation, by sending their money abroad. Governments try to prevent such flight by imposing capital controls, but they need to act quickly. Investors will anticipate the introduction of capital controls by indulging in capital flight. Infamously done by British Pop musicians who tried to flee high tax rates in the UK in 1960's and 1970's.

Capital gains tax

A tax levied when investors sell assets for more than the purchase price. Some economists argue that such taxes discourage risk-taking. But if capital gains are tax-free, and income is taxable, that creates a potential incentive; ingenious accountants will find ways to transform income into capital gains. In Canada, tax free capital gains are 50%. The other 50% is subject to taxation at an Individuals marginal tax rate.

Capital goods

Physical assets that company use in the manufacturing process.

Capital markets

Dual meaning. Those markets where governments, companies and other institutions raise long-term money in the form of equities or stock and bonds. By contrast, the term "money markets" is used for the places where short-term finance is raised.

Capitalism

A term coined to describe the use of private capital to finance economic activity. Investors and businesspersons use their money to create businesses, hiring workers, renting property, and buying equipment as needed. Any surplus, or profit, belongs to the entrepreneur or investors. Communism is seen as the obverse of capitalism, as all economic activity is controlled by the state.

Carbon tax

A tax levied on carbon emissions. The aim is to penalise heavy emitters and encourage alternative approaches that do not contribute to global warming.

Cartel

Agreement where a group of producers collaborate to fix the price, or restrict the supply, of a good or service. Perhaps the best-known example is the Organisation of the Petroleum Exporting Countries. (OPEC).

Central bank

The institution at the heart of a country's financial system. It has many roles. Traditionally, it sets the level of short-term interest rates through its interactions with commercial banks. It uses rate changes to control inflation and affect the level of economic output. Since 2009 many central banks have attempted to affect long-term interest rates through quantitative easing. The central bank acts as a lender of last resort to protect the financial system from collapse. As shown by the Great financial crisis of 2008 -2009. Central banks also control foreign exchange reserves and can use these to intervene in the currency markets.

Classical economics

The dominant school of thought in the late 18th and 19th centuries, first developed by Adam Smith. It largely focused on the self-correcting nature of economies if left alone by governments and thus argued for the 'invisible hand' or Laissez faire approach and, thanks in part to the theory of comparative advantage, a belief in free trade.

Collateral

An item pledged as security against a loan. An obvious example is a house, which homeowners used as collateral when taking out a mortgage. In financial markets, safe securities such as Treasury bonds are often used as collateral by traders and investors.

Commercial Banks

These Institutions are the core of the financial system. Commercial Banks take in deposits and make loans, thereby creating money. In a crisis, banks may cease lending (or insist on the repayment of past loans) causing immense economic damage. The Great Financial Crisis in 2008-2009 is a prime example of Banks capping individuals Line of Credits to "balances already accrued". Investment Banks are an arm of Commercial Banking and advise on transactions such as acquisitions and mergers, IPO's and in financial assets such as bonds and shares.

Commodity

A raw material, such as palladium, oil or copper, that is usually traded in bulk. Changes in commodity prices can have significant economic effects by, for example, feeding through into consumer prices. A sharp rise in energy prices can adversely affect consumer demand; because consumers must spend more on energy, they have less to spend elsewhere. Evident by the recent Russian invasion of Ukraine. Natural gas prices in Europe skyrocketed as measures were taken to limit the supply of natural gas from Russia.

Commodity cycle

A pattern of rising and falling commodity prices and production. Rising commodity prices cause consumers to cut back their use and producers to expand output. In the ensuing glut, prices fall and output falls until commodities are so cheap that their use rises again.

Communism

A system, devised by Karl Marx, in which the state controls virtually all economic activity. Private property is outlawed, and income inequality is reduced. The theory is idealistic; in practice, communist regimes have been highly authoritarian.

Competition

A concept at the heart of economics. Firms compete to sell the best goods and services to consumers, and to attract the best workers. The aim is to allocate resources in the most efficient manner.

Conglomerate

A large company that has diversified across a range of countries and business areas, normally through making acquisitions.

Consumer confidence

A measure, taken from a survey, of the public's attitude towards the economic outlook. If people are worried about their jobs, or political unrest, or a pandemic, they will be less likely to spend money.

Consumer prices index

A measure of the cost of a "typical" assortment of goods and services, used to calculate the rate of inflation. Statisticians first calculate the composition of the basket of goods and services bought by the average consumer: e.g., bread, oil and electrical goods. They then compare the cost of those goods in one period with that in another, weighting the goods and services to reflect the amount the average consumer spends. The change in this consumer prices index over the period (e.g., a year) is the inflation rate.

Consumption

The spending of money on goods and services by households. Consumers can either spend their income or save it. When consumers are cautious, they spend less and save more. This can have adverse economic effects as consumption is usually the largest component of aggregate demand.

Cost-benefit analysis

A process of assessing the feasibility and profitability of a public-sector project or business decision. As the name suggests, all the potential costs are compared with the potential revenues and other benefits. Although the idea is sound, the estimates are subject to a lot of uncertainty. Budget overruns are common.

Coupon

Term given to the rate of return or interest rate on a bond, which stems from a time in history when physical coupons were attached to bond certificates. On a fixed-rate bond, the coupon does not change but the price of the bond does; the yield of the bond is determined by the relationship between the coupon and the price, plus any capital gain or loss that would result in holding the bond until it matures. Otherwise known as the 'yield to maturity'.

Credit

A catch-all term for the extension of loans to individuals, companies or organisations. The term is also used more generally to refer to the total amount of debt in an economy.

Credit crunch.

A sudden reduction in the willingness of banks and others to lend money. This usually has adverse economic consequences such as the 2008-2010 timeframe.

Credit default swap

A derivative contract between two parties in which one insures the other against the default of a bond or loan. One of the products at the heart of the 2007-09 financial crisis.

Credit expansion.

An increase in the willingness of banks and others to lend money. This normally happens during an economic boom. If credit expands too fast, this can be a sign of excessive speculation, often in the property market.

Creditor

A person or institution that is owed money.

Cryptocurrency

Tokens created digitally. Enthusiasts see the currencies as a way of avoiding fiat currency and the oversight of governments and banks; ownership and transfer are recorded in a distributed ledger, called the blockchain. The value of cryptocurrencies has been highly volatile, making it difficult for them to be either a store of value or medium of exchange, two essential functions of a conventional currency. We see by the lack of regulation that dishonesty rules and the market of crypto is perfect for proceeds of crime.

Currency

> The monetary unit of a nation state, or group of states. Examples are the Canadian and US dollar, the euro and the Japanese yen. In the modern era, most currencies are allowed to rise and fall in value against each other and are traded in the foreign exchange market.

Currency peg

> A system in which a national currency is fixed in relation to another currency (usually the US dollar). In the modern era, this tends to be done by a developing country with a history of inflation and currency depreciation; the peg is supposedly a way of imposing some measured discipline. Maintaining the peg leads to pain in the form of high interest rates and recession, so the link is abandoned.

Current account

> This measures all the non-financial transactions between a country and the rest of the world—chiefly its imports and exports of goods and services—and transfers such as remittances and financial aid. Since the balance of payments must balance, a current account deficit necessitates a capital account surplus (described as an inflow of money) to balance it.

Debt

> Money borrowed from someone else, whether a bank, a company, or a person.

Default

> When a borrower fails to repay a debt. Widespread defaults are problematic since they can lead to a collapse in the banking system.

Deflation

> Falling prices across an entire economy. Deflationary years were quite common under the gold standard when prices were stable over the long run, with some up and some down years. But deflation tends to be a problem in the modern era since it tends to be associated with falling nominal incomes. Since debt repayments are fixed in nominal terms, deflation often leads to a crisis as debtors struggle to repay their loans.

Demographics

> Characteristics of a population, such as size or composition by age. Demographics and demographic change can influence economic growth; if there are more people of working age, growth is likely to be stronger.

Dependency ratio

> The proportion of the population that is not of working age, compared with that which could work, if it chose to. Conventionally, dependants are defined as those aged up to 14 or over 65. Sometimes the figures are separated into youth dependency and old-age dependency. The higher the ratio, the greater the tax burden that is likely to fall on the working population; this is a problem for many developed economies, given the numbers now surviving into old age. Baby boomers are accounting for a larger proportion of health costs and lower tax revenue as they retire in western society.

Deposit insurance

A program whereby a government agrees to compensate depositors if a bank goes bust. This can help prevent bank runs when depositors panic. In Canada, CDIC insurance protects member organizations.

Depreciation

Means different things in business and economics. In the foreign exchange markets, this means a decline in the value of a currency, e.g., "the British pound depreciated by 10% against the dollar". In accounting, this relates to the gradual decline in the value of an asset, due to wear and tear. Companies depreciate their assets over their lifetime; this will show up as a deduction on the income account and a reduction in the value of assets on the balance sheet.

Depression

A prolonged and sharp fall in economic output, associated with a high level of unemployment. The Great Depression of the 1930s is the still the most notable example.

Deregulation

It is a staple of conservative thought that there are too many regulations which hold back economic growth. So, every few years, governments announce a policy of deregulation to cut back the red tape. It turns out, however, that public opinion often demands that governments act to ban things that are bad, or that are disliked. And so more regulations are introduced.

Derivatives

Financial assets whose value "derives" from something else, such as a stock market index or a commodity price. Examples are futures, options, and swaps. Derivatives are often used to insure against a sudden change in the value of a key variable, such as a sharp rise in the oil price. But they can also be used to speculate on price movements.

Devaluation

A formal reduction in the value of a currency. This occurs when a country has a fixed exchange rate and decides to alter the rate.

Developed countries.

A term used for nations where incomes per person are high, relative to the global average. These countries tended to industrialise early and are mainly based in Europe, and in former European settler colonies in North America and Australasia. Many Asian nations such as Japan and South Korea are also classified as developed. Can also be classified as mature economies.

Developing countries

A term used to describe countries where income per person is lower than in "developed nations". These countries will usually have industrialised later than those in Europe or America. There is no official designation of developing countries and the World Bank uses the terms "lower-middle" and "low-income". Also, as they grow, they may be classified as emerging economies.

Diminishing returns

Production involves certain inputs such as labour, machinery, and raw materials. At first, adding more inputs will improve productivity substantially; but eventually the marginal gains from adding more inputs (costs increase) will reduce. This is the law of diminishing returns.

Direct taxes

Taxes collected directly by the government. Examples include income tax and corporate profits tax. As opposed to indirect taxation.

Discount rate

The rate the US Federal Reserve or Bank of Canada charges for lending to commercial banks. In addition, a discount rate is used by any investor or company trying to calculate the present value of a series of future cashflows. Since money in the future is worth less than money today, these cashflows must be reduced or discounted. The chosen discount rate, usually related to current interest rates or bond yields, can make a big difference to the time value of money and net present value.

Disinflation

A situation where prices across the economy are rising, but more slowly than before—e.g., a fall in the annual inflation rate from 10% to 5%. Not to be confused with deflation which is when hen consumer and asset prices decrease over time and purchasing power increases. Essentially, you can buy more goods or services tomorrow with the same amount of money you have today.

Diversification

The practice of spreading one's interests widely. In investment, diversification is considered best practice: a big Mutual fund will own equities in a wide range of companies, across many nations, and will own bonds and property as well. Companies will also diversify across nations.

Dividend

A regular payment made by a company to its shareholders. The payment comes from a company's profits. Normally companies try to increase dividends over time; when they cut the dividend, this is a sign of trouble.

Division of labour

One of the fundamental principles of economics. Work can be undertaken more efficiently if broken up into discrete tasks. It is also more efficient for individuals to focus on their own jobs and use their wages to purchase goods and services, rather than attempt to grow their own food, build their own home and make their own cars.

Duopoly

A situation where two producers control a market.

CHAPTER 2

ECONOMIC Terms E — H

ESG investing

The initials stand for "environmental", "social" and "corporate governance". The amount of money devoted to ESG investing increased substantially in the second decade of the 21st century and is linked more broadly to belief in a green economy. Supporters said that companies which neglected these issues would eventually be unprepared for the face of regulation, consumer backlash and scandal.

Economically inactive

A term generally used to cover people of working age (generally 15 to 64 years old) who are not seeking a job, nor in full-time education. This includes people who are caring for relatives, those who are too sick to work, those who have retired before the state pension age and "discouraged workers" who have given up trying for a job.

Economies of scale

The owner of a firm needs to buy machinery, rent property, and so on. Some of these costs are fixed. As the firm produces more, these costs are spread over more units; the average cost of production falls. These economies of scale mean that mass production tends to result in cheaper goods.

Elasticity

A measure of the responsiveness of one variable to changes in another. For example, if a good rises in price by 10%, then demand could fall by less than 10% (price inelasticity) or more than 10% (price elasticity). Essential goods like food and fuel tend to be price inelastic.

Emerging markets

A term, largely used in investment circles, for developing countries that lagged the Industrial revolution in Europe and colonial conquests. Investors might put their capital into emerging markets because they believe the growth prospects for such countries (and thus the returns on equities) will be higher. But emerging markets tend to be risky and politically unstable and can suffer from capital flight when investors become risk averse.

Endowment effect

A psychological bias that causes people to be more willing to retain an object than acquire the same object if they don't own it. Put another way, they value an object they won more highly than the market value. This may explain behaviour that is not "rational" in economic terms.

Entrepreneur

Individual who puts together the factors of production (labour, machinery, business) to find a new business. Entrepreneurs tend to be much praised as risk-takers who boost economic growth and is the backbone of a capitalistic economy.

Equilibrium

One of the important concepts in economics. Equilibrium means a balance between the supply of and demand for a good at a market-clearing price.

Equity

Long-term capital raised from investors in the form of shares. The shareholders are the owners of the company and share in its assets and profits; to take over a company, a rival must make an offer that satisfies its shareholders. In normal circumstances, equity is never repaid as opposed to debt. Shareholders have voting rights (over issues such as the appointment of directors) and will sometimes receive income in the form of dividends.

Euro zone

Those countries within the European Union that have adopted the euro as their currency. In addition, six non-EU countries (Andorra, Kosovo, Monaco, Montenegro, San Marino, and the Vatican City) use the currency. Monetary policy in the euro zone is set by the European Central Bank.

Exchange rate

The rate at which one currency is exchanged for another. Generally, this is either a fixed or floating rate.

Exports

Goods and services sold to foreign buyers. When a foreign tourist buys a meal in France, that counts as a French export.

Externality

An externality is a cost or benefit to a third party because of someone else's actions. Externalities lie outside the market system. Polluted air, caused by a chemical plant's emissions, is a negative externality.

Factors of production

The ingredients necessary for economic activity which tend to be land, labour, capital and the entrepreneurship needed to bring the elements together.

Fair trade

An approach which argues that consumers should not simply focus on the cost of the goods they buy but on the working conditions and wages of the workers that supply them. Various schemes offer to certify that a product (such as coffee) has been made in a fair-trade fashion. There is much backlash now from goods made in countries that use child labour.

Federal Reserve System US

The most powerful actor in the global financial system. Set up in 1913, America's central bank divides the country into 12 Reserve districts, each with its own regional Federal Reserve bank. These are overseen by the Federal Reserve Board.

Fiat currency

A currency declared to be legal tender in a country by a government. Such a currency is not backed by gold or another asset; the government simply issues an order (or fiat) that it is legal tender and can insist it be used to pay taxes. Most countries have fiat currencies, and they achieve widespread acceptance as a medium of exchange because of their convenience.

Financial markets

The places where money is invested, in the form of bonds, equities, derivatives and short-term loans.

Fiscal drag

A way in which inflation can boost tax revenues. In most tax systems, workers must earn a certain amount before they pay income tax or pay it a higher rate. If those allowances are not uprated every year in line with inflation, workers end up paying more in tax in real terms when their wages rise.

Fiscal policy

Decisions relating to the amount a government raises in taxes and spends on public services. Fiscal tightening means the government is raising taxes or cutting spending (or both) and thus taking demand out of the economy. Fiscal easing means the government is lowering taxes or raising spending (or both) and thus adding demand.

Fixed costs

Costs of production that do not change when output changes, for example the rent paid on a factory.

Fixed exchange rate

When the value of one currency is tied to that of another or (in the past) to gold. Fixed exchange rates were common until the 1970s as they offered certainties; importers knew the cost of goods bought from abroad; exporters knew the value of the revenues they would receive for selling goods to foreigners. But they proved difficult to maintain as capital flowed more freely across national boundaries.

Fixed rate

When the interest rate on a bond, or other financial instrument, is invariable.

Floating exchange rate

When a currency's value moves freely against that of other countries. Floating rates have been widespread since the 1970s after the weakening of capital controls.

Foreign direct investment (FDI)

When a foreign investor sets up a new operation in a country or buys an existing business. FDI is distinct from portfolio investment, the purchase of a small stake in a business by a pension fund or sovereign wealth fund. FDI can boost productivity, by bringing new technology and upgrading the skills of domestic workers.

Foreign exchange market

The forum where currencies are traded. Often abbreviated to FX or forex.

Foreign exchange reserves

Assets, normally held by a central bank, that can be used in a financial crisis or to influence the country's exchange rate. Central banks tend to hold their reserves in major currencies like the dollar or euro, as well as gold.

Framing

In behavioural economics, the idea that how a proposition is framed can affect the reaction of individuals. So, expressing the cost of an annual subscription at $72 a year will attract fewer customers than describing it as $6 a month. Or pricing a car for sale at $9,990 makes it more appealing than $10,000 even.

Free trade

Free-trade believers insist that the unfettered international exchange of goods and services leads to more efficient economies and thus, in the long run, greater prosperity for all. Opponents argue that workers in domestic industries lose their jobs when exposed to international trade, and this leads many governments to adopt tariff and other protectionist policies.

Free trade area

Region or regions which has dropped tariffs and quotas and other controls on import and export activity. The best-known examples are the European Union and NAFTA (now the USMCA).

Free-market economists

Those who believe that the market is better at allocating resources than governments and that excessive regulation and high public spending tend to diminish growth in the long run.

Frictional unemployment

The joblessness that results from people quitting their jobs in search of better opportunities or that occurs as struggling firms shed labour and rising firms hunt for new workers.

Full employment

When everyone who wants a job at prevailing wages can find one. Zero unemployment is not possible since companies go bust, or shed labour, and it can take time for workers to find a new job. Central banks and governments may aim to achieve full employment, but it is usually defined at 2-4% as this reflects reality.

Future

A contract, traded on an exchange, to trade a commodity, or a financial instrument, at a future date. Futures can be used to hedge or insure against a price change (for example, a farmer might sell his crop in advance) or to speculate on a future price change.

General Agreement on Tariffs and Trade

The General Agreement on Tariffs and Trade or GATT was signed in 1947 and aimed to eliminate the protectionism that had plagued the global economy in the 1930s. It was followed by several rounds of negotiations which gradually reduced trade barriers and was eventually superseded in the 1990s by the World Trade Organization or WTO.

Gig economy

A term given to workers whose jobs are part-time or temporary, and who thus lack job security. Many people work for the new wave of companies that have emerged in the 21st century such as Uber. As contractors, gig-economy workers have few rights such as holiday pay or pensions, although courts have ruled that some must be treated as conventional employees.

Globalisation

The tendency for national economies to become integrated with each other, through the movement of goods and services, capital, and people. The first modern wave of globalisation in the late 19th century was ended by the first world war. A second stage emerged during the late 20th century as China, and the ex-communist countries of eastern Europe, joined the global trading system. With recent extreme political movements to the right, we are witnessing efforts to 'de-globalize". War in Ukraine has highlighted this in 2024. As an example, Germany is dependent on energy needs from Russia, an end user market for its products in China and its defense needs handled by the US. Prompting calls for less dependence on these factors.

Gold

Precious metal that was once a central part of the global monetary system. Central banks still hold gold as part of their reserves. Some see the metal, which is limited in supply, as a hedge against inflation, although its record in that respect is patchy.

Gold standard

An international system, used in the 20th centuries, that linked the amount of domestic currency in circulation (and the exchange rate) to a country's gold reserves. Since these reserves grew slowly, so did the money supply and there was little long-term inflation. This protected the interests of creditors, but it meant that any competitive adjustment in the economy involved painful deflation. As a result, the world abandoned the standard in the 1930s.

Government bonds

Debt issued by governments is often the most important instrument in a country's financial markets. Because most governments can be relied upon to repay the debt, it is regarded as a risk-free asset and is a core part of a portfolio.

Gravity model of trade

The theory that the intensity of trade between two countries is dependent on two factors; their economic size and their distance from one another. In 2021 America's top three trading partners were Canada and Mexico (its nearest neighbours) and China (the world's second-largest economy or first based on PPP calculations).

Great Depression

The era in the 1930s when economic output and volumes of international trade collapsed. Led to the adoption of a more Keynesian economic approach after the second world war.

Gross domestic product (GDP)

The main measure of an economy's size. GDP is calculated from the market value of all the finished goods and services within a country's borders over a set period.

Gross national product (GNP)

An alternative to GDP, GNP is the value of all goods and services produced by citizens of a country, both domestically and internationally. Income earned by foreign residents is deducted.

Hedge funds

Investment vehicles that attract money from institutions such as pension funds and wealthy individuals. They follow a wide range of strategies, often using leverage or margins and going short (betting on falling prices). As well as an annual management fee, they charge a performance fee; individual hedge-fund managers can become very wealthy themselves.

Hedging

This occurs when individuals, companies and institutions try to protect themselves against adverse market movements, such as changes in commodity prices, currencies, or interest rates.

Hot money

Short-term capital that flows into a country in search of quick returns. Hot money tends to flow through the banks, leading to a lending spree that causes speculation in the property market. In Canada, we see foreign influences in buying properties and driving prices up. It also drives up the country's currency, making life more difficult for its exports. When sentiment turns, hot money flows out and may cause a currency to slump and bursting any speculative bubbles.

Human capital

The skills and brainpower of workers. Improving human capital through training and education is often seen as a way of improving productivity.

Hybrid working

A term that emerged during the Covid pandemic to describe employees who work part of the time in the office and part of the time at home. This appeals to many workers, as it reduces commuting time, while also being acceptable to companies since employees still come in to attend meetings and interact with their managers and colleagues.

Hyperinflation

When inflation gets out of control—as happened, for example, in Germany post-World War 1. A loaf of bread cost 200bn marks in November 1923 and workers were paid twice a day because their wages fell in value during the day. Such high rates of inflation are fuelled by rapid expansion of the money supply.

Hypothecated taxes

The earmarking of tax revenues for a specific purpose, such as roadbuilding. Hypothecation can be a way of making tax rises more politically acceptable, but governments often find a way of diverting the revenues to other departments.

Hysteresis

A term borrowed from physics, where it refers to a lagged effect. In economics, it is used to describe persistent phenomena, such as the continuation of high levels of unemployment, even when an economy has recovered; workers may have lost enthusiasm or seen their skills decline.

CHAPTER 3
ECONOMIC Terms I—N

Illiquid assets

Assets that cannot readily be tuned into cash or can only be sold quickly at a substantial discount. Illiquid assets are often the cause of financial crises when entities like banks have a mismatch between their liabilities (customers' deposits, which can be instantly withdrawn) and their assets (long-term loans, which are illiquid). Illiquid assets will often offer a higher return because of their greater risk.

Imports

Goods and services made in another country and brought into the local economy.

Income

The (regular) flow of money to the factors of production. Labour receives wages; land receives rent; capital receives profits, interest, and dividends.

Income tax

A reliable way of raising revenue for governments. Income tax is deducted by the employer before workers receive their pay. Most governments don't levy tax until individual incomes have reached a minimum level and tax higher incomes at higher rates.

Indexation

This term is most used to describe the linking of a variable to the inflation rate. Some governments link benefits to inflation or a "cost of living adjustment'. Several governments have issued government bonds of which the coupon and repayment value rise in line with inflation; these are known as index-linked bonds. Indexation also refers to a field of fund management that attempts to replicate the performance of a stock-market index.

Indirect taxation

Tax collected by an entity other than the government. Examples include sales tax (collected by retailers), levies on alcohol and tobacco, and taxes on tourism (collected by hotels and airlines).

Industrial policy

The promotion of what a government considers to be strategic industries such as computer and defense related. The disruption of supply chains during and after the covid-19 pandemic, concerns about the rise of Chinese economic power, and the Russian invasion of Ukraine have given industrial policy a new lease of life in the West. The widespread adoption of subsidies and tariffs other measures to promote favoured industries raises renewed protectionism.

Inflation

A general rise in the price level. This is normally calculated by comparing the price of a basket of goods (measured by a consumer price index) at different times and can be used as a measure of the cost of living. Central banks often have a mandate to control inflation and may look at a wide range of gauges to understand the underlying trend; for example, measures of "core" inflation that exclude volatile items such as food and energy.

Inflation targeting

In the modern era, governments in many countries have asked central banks to target a specific rate of, or range for, for inflation and given them independence from political control of their operations. Inflation-targeting central banks have used various tools of monetary policy, such as changes in interest rates and/or quantitative easing. A normal inflation target is in the 2-3% range.

Infrastructure

The brick and mortar of the economy. Roads, railways, airports, Electrical grid, Oil pipe delivery and container ports are all vital for an economy's operation.

Inheritance taxes

Levies on the assets of those who die most notably in the US. Governments also create exemptions to prevent small business and farms from being broken up on the owner's death.

Innovation

Innovation is a key element in improving productivity, which in turn is a big driver of economic growth. In the modern era, innovation tends to be associated with new gadgets and technology. But it can be a new way of organising work, such as Henry Ford's mass production line or the increase in Robotic and automation manufacturing. Innovation can arise from the insight of entrepreneurs and research and development.

Insider trading

The use of non-public information to gain an advantage in financial markets. It is illegal in many countries because it discriminates against other investors and can cause confidence in the probity of financial markets to fall. Usually, persons inside of affected companies can sell or buy with knowledge unknown to the general populace.

Institutional investors

A catch-all term to describe some of the major investors like insurance companies and pension funds.

Insurance

The act of protecting yourself against the financial impact of risk. Traditionally, insurance was developed to cover fire, the sinking or seizure of a ship, or the death of the family breadwinner. Insurance companies attempted to calculate the likelihood of such risks occurring.

Intangible asset

Something without physical form that can create value. Examples include intellectual property, patents, and brand names.

Intellectual property

An asset created solely by human intelligence and creativity. Examples include copyrights, patents, and trademarks.

Interest on reserves

The return paid by central banks on reserves held by commercial banks. These interest payments help to keep market interest rates at the desired level.

Interest rates

The return for lending money, and the cost of borrowing it. The level of interest rates depends on factors like inflation and geopolitical risk, credit risk of the borrower and the time value of money. Short-term rates are generally set by, or are closely linked to, the decisions of the country's central bank.

Internal rate of return

A measure used by businesses to calculate the profitability of a potential investment.

International Monetary Fund (IMF)

One of the institutions set up after the Bretton Woods agreement. It is the international body that countries turn to when in financial difficulties.

Internet

The internet, a system which connects electronic devices such as personal computers, has clearly transformed the global economy, changing the way many people work, communicate and shop.

Investment

This term is used in two linked ways, both referring to putting money to work, usually for the long term. Business investment occurs when companies buy new machines or build new factories. Portfolio investment occurs when individuals or institutions put money into long-term assets such as equities, bonds and real estate.

Investment banks

Institutions that make their money from advising corporate clients, and from trading assets, rather than from taking in deposits and making loans (like a commercial bank).

Investment management

A sector that focuses on managing the money of others. Most charge an annual fee but some also add a performance fee.

Junk bonds

Bonds that are deemed to be highly risky where the borrower might stop paying interest or default on repayment altogether. They offer a high yield as compensation for that risk.

Keynesian economics

John Maynard Keynes, a British academic and government official, changed the field of economics. Under Classical economics, governments did little to manage the economic cycle, which they believed would right itself. Governments, rather than balance their budgets, could borrow to spend money and this spending would revive demand.

Labour

A term used for both a factor for production and for the organised representatives of the working classes (trade unions and some political parties). The supply of labour is an important determinant of economic growth, and the shrinking of the working-age population in developed countries—and China—may be a limiting factor on growth in coming decades. Improving the skills of the workforce and enticing reluctant workers back into jobs is vital.

Lagged effect

The time taken for economic policy changes to affect the economy. Changes in interest rates, for example, can take as much as 18 months to have their full impact, as rates may only change when loan terms are renegotiated. The danger is that, by the time the policy starts to work, economic circumstances have changed.

Laissez-faire

This French term refers to the idea that governments should leave the economy alone as much as possible and should allow free trade.

Land

One of the factors of production. Land is in fixed supply as making up 25% of the globe's surface.

Leading indicators

Economic data that are examined for clues to coming trends. Surveys of consumer confidence, for example, may provide a pointer to the outlook for retail sales; inflation in producer prices may herald changes in consumer inflation. Some view the stock market as a leading indicator of the economic outlook.

Lender of last resort

A crucial role played by central banks during financial crises. There can be moments when depositors and creditors lose faith in the banking system, with the risk that the banks will collapse. By acting as lender of last resort to banks that would be solvent in the medium term, a central bank can reduce the economic damage.

Leverage

Investing, or speculating, with borrowed money or by putting down only a small part of the purchase price. For example, a company or an individual may buy another using a small amount of its own cash, and a larger amount of debt in the form of bank loan. The greater the proportion of debt, the higher the leverage, or gearing. Another use of leverage is to buy equities on margin. Financial crises often have excessive leverage at their heart.

Leveraged buyout

A corporate takeover, usually undertaken by a private equity group, using a lot of borrowed money. The aim is to cut costs and sell assets at the target company, thereby bringing down the debt, and making it possible for the private equity group to make a profit for its investors.

Liabilities

Something owed to others, and the other side of the balance sheet from assets. Often, this is in the form of money, such as a debt.

Liberalisation

In economic terms, this usually refers to reducing the role of the government, and the restrictions on the private sector by cutting regulations.

Limited liability

One of the most important concepts in modern capitalism. Limited liability means that investors who own the equity of a company can only lose their initial stake if the business collapses; creditors cannot pursue their other assets, such as their homes. By limiting liabilities in this way, more entrepreneurs are willing to take the risk of setting up businesses, and more investors are willing to back them.

Liquidity

The quality of being easily turned into cash. This can depend on the nature of the instrument. Treasury Bills is short-term debt issued by the American government, are cash-like instruments.

Loss aversion

A psychological trait, that dislikes the acceptance of losses. Investors may hold on to losing positions, rather than sell them, because they are unwilling to recognise their mistake.

Macroeconomics

The analysis of how the overall economy works; how the decisions of consumers, business, investors, and governments affect key measures such as GDP, unemployment, and Inflation. Economists try to use macroeconomic analysis to forecast economic indicators, but human behaviour is hard to predict, especially as forecasts can affect individual decisions. Macroeconomic policy tools include both monetary and fiscal policy.

Manufacturing

The process of making physical products from raw materials using labour and machinery. Once dominant in developed economies, it now takes a smaller share of GDP now.

Margin

Used in both economics and finance. In the stock market, investors and analysts often focus on profit margins; the difference between the revenues from selling a product and the costs of producing it, often expressed as a percentage of the latter. Investors can also buy shares on margin, putting up only a fraction of the overall cost.

Marginal cost

The cost of producing an extra unit of something. When production is increased, the marginal cost of producing an extra item can be significantly lower than the average cost of production.

Marginal propensity to consume.

The proportion of an extra earned dollar that an individual would spend rather than save. People with lower incomes have a higher marginal propensity to consume than the rich.

Marginal tax rate

The proportion of an extra earned dollar that will be taken by tax. High marginal tax rates can reduce incentives to work. This occurs at both ends of the income scale.

Mass production

One of the breakthroughs in 20th-century manufacturing was the development of mass production, normally associated first with the Ford Motor Company. Mass production usually involved the division of labour, specialised machinery, and standardised products. These economies of scale allowed manufacturers to lower their prices and vastly expand the potential market for their goods.

Maturity

A term which applies to debt and refers to the amount of life before the debt needs to be repaid and thus refinanced.

Mergers and acquisitions

This term, often abbreviated to M&A, concerns corporate takeovers. Genuine mergers, in which two companies of roughly equal size combine, are much rarer than acquisitions, in which a larger company buys a smaller one. And hostile acquisitions, in which the smaller company resists the deal, are rarer than agreed takeovers.

Microeconomics

A path of economics that studies the decision-making of individual entities, such as individuals and businesses. Microeconomists look at how these agents will respond to incentives, or to changes in prices, regulations, or taxes.

Minimum wage

An hourly pay rate for workers, set by law, with the aim of reducing poverty and protecting workers from exploitation. Many economists were historically dubious about the benefits of a minimum wage believing it would reduce demand for labour and thus drive-up unemployment.

Mixed economy

An economic system that combines elements of free enterprise and state planning. Few economies are not mixed to some degree.

Models

Economic relationships in mathematical or graphical form, designed to allow hypotheses to be tested. Inevitably, models must simplify the incredibly complex nature of relationships in the real world.

Monetary policy

Used by the central bank with the use of interest rates and other tools to try to influence the economy. Interest rates are raised when the bank is trying to control inflation and lowered when inflation is low, and it is trying to revive the economy. The financial crisis of 2007-09 led central banks to lower rates to Zero.

Money

Money can be any token that is accepted as payment. Money used to be linked to precious metals, but modern money is largely fiat currency and is electronic in form. Whatever its form, money needs to be a reasonably stable store of value and an acceptable medium of exchange.

Money markets

A term used to describe the borrowing and lending of money on a short-term basis (generally for less than a year). Banks need to finance themselves with short-term borrowing on a regular basis.

Money supply

The total amount of money in an economy. Notes and coins are only a small part of the money we use. Current account balances, unused credit card balances and holdings of money-market funds can all be added to the mix.

Monopoly

A company with a controlling position in an industry or sector. Traditionally, the main fear was that monopolies would exploit their position to overcharge customers.

Moral hazard

The risk that providing insurance might alter the behaviour of those being insured. Homeowners or car drivers may take more risks if they know that an insurance company will cover their losses. This is also a problem for central banks when they act as a lender of last resort; knowing they will be rescued in a crisis, bank executives may take more risks.

Multiplier effect

This concept relates to the proportional increase, or decrease, in demand that can arise from an injection, or withdrawal, of spending. So, a government increase in spending on, say, roadbuilding will mean more jobs for workers who spend their wages on other goods and services, which encourages the employment of more workers, and so on.

NAFTA (North American Free Trade Agreement)

A deal signed in 1993 by America, Canada, and Mexico to eliminate tariff barriers between the three countries by creating a zone of free trade. It was renamed the US-Mexico-Canada Agreement (USMCA).

National debt

The sum of government debt, usually expressed as a proportion of GDP.

Nationalisation

The takeover by the state of private businesses. Under Communism, all large businesses are state-owned, and the previous private owners are rarely compensated. In a social democracy, the state tends to focus on certain industries, notably utilities (power generation, water etc.), those deemed to be strategically important (steel, oil) and loss-making businesses that employ a lot of workers.

Negative equity

This arises when a borrower buys a property and the price falls sharply, so that the size of the loan is greater than the value of the property. Also called being underwater. This was a big problem in the American housing market in the 2007-20010 timeframe. Negative equity meant, at best, borrowers would be unable to move and at worst, they would default, with resulting losses for the lenders as well as themselves.

Negative income tax

A payment made to people on low incomes as a way of reducing poverty. In Canada there is the GIS (Guaranteed Supplemental Income) to help seniors. The approach can be an alternative to welfare payments, which can be complex to administer and carry social stigma. Instead, the state just makes a payment to those whose incomes are below a certain level.

Negative interest rates

A modern development that would have surprised economists from earlier eras, negative rates mean that investors are in effect charged for lending, or depositing, their money. They emerged in the wake of the 2007-09 financial crisis, as Central Banks found new ways to ease monetary policy. Investors had a few reasons for tolerating negative yields including facing bigger losses investing elsewhere.

Nominal interest rates

The stated level of interest rates but not accounting for inflationary trends. A nominal return of 3% might sound good, but if inflation is 6%, then the purchasing value of the saver's money is declining (by about 3%). Real interest rates adjust for actual or expected inflation.

CHAPTER 4
ECONOMIC Terms O-R

OPEC

The Organisation of Petroleum Exporting Countries is an oil producer's cartel which attempts to influence both the supply and the price of oil. It was most effective in the 1970s, quadrupling the oil price and contributing to stagflation at that time. The influence and effects have propelled new producers like Norway and America to develop its own shale oil reserves. But OPEC's decisions still matter.

Offshore haven

A jurisdiction which imposes little or no tax on transactions or profits and thus is chosen by financial and multinational companies as a hub for some of their activities. Rich individuals also hold money offshore, to reduce their tax bills.

Oligopoly

When a few firms control a market. This can lead to agreements (tacit or explicit) to fix prices or exclude new entrants. As an extension of Communism, the term, Oligarchy is a power structure most famous in Russia where power rests with the few. Politicians and select businesspeople enjoy massive economic benefits when the general populace are oppressed and unable to fight against this.

Opportunity cost

The cost of something may not just be its price but the alternative; what was given up getting it. So, the opportunity cost of spending the afternoon shopping is the wages you might have earned had you stayed at work. Or just saving those dollars you spent.

Optimal currency area

A theoretical assessment of the geopolitical regions where it would be most efficient, in economic terms, to share one currency. The criteria include the existence of highly integrated economies, with flexible labour markets, and the potential for fiscal transfers between nations. The European Union has applied the EURO as its sole currency and have had measured success.

Option

A derivative contract that gives the right, but not the obligation, to undertake a transaction at a set price for a set period. A call option is the right to buy and a put option the right to sell. In return, the option holder pays a premium to the person who grants the option.

Overheating

If an economy is growing too fast, companies may face bottlenecks in acquiring resources or hiring labour. This will lead to higher costs and wages, and thus rising inflation.

Passive management

The purchase of a portfolio that replicates the broad market in an asset class like stocks. Passive management emerged because many active managers failed to beat the index after fees.

Pension funds

Institutional Investment companies that run portfolios on behalf of employed persons and retirees. Final-salary (or defined-benefit) and/or Defined contribution funds offer a pension that is linked to employees' salaries; these are increasingly confined to the public sector.

Phillips curve

This concept suggests that inflation and unemployment are inversely related; when inflation is high, unemployment is low and vice versa. In the 1970s, however, both inflation and unemployment were high (see stagflation) and in the 2000s, both were low by historical standards. This suggests the relationship is far from stable.

Platform company

A new type of firm that emerged with the internet and links together suppliers and consumers. For example, Airbnb connects homeowners with properties to rent and holidaymakers who need somewhere to stay. Platform companies benefit from social media and network effects.

Price

The cost of a good or service set by the balance or equilibrium of supply and demand.

Price-earnings ratio

An oft-used valuation method for individual shares and for the equities market. It compares the share price with the company's after-tax profits.

Private sector

Those economic activities not controlled by the government, ranging from a one-man insurance operation to giant corporations.

Privatisation

The transfer of assets or firms from the public sector to the private sector. There was much enthusiasm for this in the 1980s and 1990s, not least because it raised money for governments in a relatively painless fashion. Some sectors, such as telecoms and airlines, clearly benefited in terms of operating efficiency from being privatised.

Productivity

As a top concept in economics, productivity measures the level of output for a given level of inputs. This is most expressed as output per worker hour. Boosting productivity is the key to long-term economic growth.

Profit

The difference between a company's revenues and its costs. Profits lie at the heart of the capitalist system and are one of the key motives for business formation. They will either be reinvested in the business or distributed to shareholders in the form of dividends or share buy-backs.

Progressive taxation

A system in which higher marginal rates of taxation apply to higher incomes.

Property

Ownership of private property is the essence of all economic systems except in Communist countries. Those who own property (and includes many forms of assets), have an incentive to use it productively and to invest it for future gains.

Protectionism

A policy that attempts to promote companies based in the home country and discriminate against those from abroad. This can be done via taxes or tariffs or via regulations that exclude imports. Protectionism is often politically popular because it appears to safeguard workers' jobs, and many companies will lobby politicians to exclude foreign competitors.

Public sector

That part of the economy, which is controlled by, or owned by, the government.

Public spending

The amount that the government spends is a significant part of most economies, ranging from 30% to 50% of GDP across many developed countries.

Purchasing-power parity (PPP)

A method of adjusting exchange rates to take account of the different levels of prices in different countries. In the absence of barriers to trade, theory suggests that the prices of goods and services in different countries should be roughly equivalent. The calculation of PPP exchange rates is a way of assessing whether currencies are under- or over-valued. In nominal dollars, the US is number one in total GDP but in PPP dollars, China is number one.

Quantitative easing (QE)

A policy introduced to alleviate the effects of the 2007-09 financial crisis. Central banks slashed intertest rates to Zero, but other measures had to be undertaken. QE involved banks buying government bonds with the purpose of injecting liquidity into the economy and pushing down bond yields.

Quantitative tightening

The opposite of Quantitative Easing. This involves shrinking the central bank's bond portfolio—either by selling bonds back to the private sector or by letting them mature and not reinvesting the proceeds—thereby removing liquidity from the economy and adding to the upward pressure on bond yields. 1n 2023-2024, quantitative tightening is in its early stages, and it seems likely that it will be a long while before QE is reversed.

Quantity theory of money

A prime point of monetarism is that the money supply is the main driver of inflationary pressures.

Quota

A trade barrier that limits the number, or monetary value, of goods that a country import.

Rate of return

The annual gain whether it be income, profit, or increased valuation from a project, expressed as a proportion of the capital put in.

Raw materials

Basic commodities and/or other inputs that firms need to manufacture products.

Real terms

An adjustment for inflationary pressures. A pay increase of 5% represents a cut in real terms if inflation is 7% but a gain in real terms if inflation is 3%. Real interest rates and real exchange rates are adjusted for inflation.

Recession

A period of falling economic output and often is defined as two consecutive quarters of declining GDP. Or more loosely it can be regarded as "a significant decline in economic activity that is spread across the economy and that lasts more than a few months".

Regressive taxes

Levies that take a larger proportion of the income of poor people than of the wealthy. Generally, sales tax is regressive, whereas income taxes are not.

Research and development

Often shortened to R&D, this is the vital work that helps to create innovation and boosts productivity in the economy. Governments can directly fund R&D themselves (particularly in wartime) or encourage it through tax breaks.

Reserve currency

A currency held by the Bank of Canada for use in emergencies. The central bank might need reserves to defend the currency of Canada (by selling the foreign currency and buying the Canadian dollars). Or it might lend its reserves to domestic banks should they need them. The dominant reserve currency is the American dollar.

Risk

The possibility that events might not turn out as expected. Risk faces all economic participants; workers might not get paid or might lose their jobs; customers may overpay or purchase a shoddy product; producers may find that demand is much lower than they hoped; investors may lose money; and so on. Some risks can be quantified: actuaries have a pretty good idea how many people will die in a normal year.

Risk premium

The extra return investors demand for holding risky assets such as equities. The risk premium needs to reflect two factors; the potential for absolute loss if the company goes bust and the variability of its price. In a crisis, risky assets plunge in price, meaning that investors may have to sell them at a loss.

Risk-averse

A state of caution which can lead to subdued economic activity. Businesses are unwilling to invest in new production facilities; banks are unwilling to lend; investors prefer the safety of the guarantees of treasury bills to any equities.

CHAPTER 5

ECONOMIC Terms S—Z

Sales tax

A much used and lucrative source of government finance, sales taxes are a form of indirect tax or user tax, as they are collected by retailers.

Sanctions

A denial of economic access designed to enforce global order. Sanctions might include trade embargoes, bans on travel and investment, and asset freezes. They have become a widely used tool of foreign policy against Iran and Russia in particular.

Savings

Income that, instead of being consumed, is set aside for future use. Savings are also vital for long-term economic growth since they provide the funds for investment.

Seasonal adjustment

Some economic activity varies depending on the time of the year. Retail sales surge in the run-up to Christmas or Black Friday. Adjusting economic data take account these variations.

Securities

A catch-all term used to describe tradable financial instruments, such as equities and bonds.

Securitisation

A practice of bundling together certain types of assets so they can be repackaged as interest-bearing securities. The assets in question tend to be those that are not normally tradable: residential mortgages, commercial mortgages, car loans etc. Securitisation was highly popular in the early 2000s, when investors were looking for assets that yielded more than government bonds. But the bundling of subprime mortgages to the great financial crisis of 2007-09.

Seniority

The order in which creditors are entitled to be repaid in the event of a company going bankrupt. Senior debt must be paid off before junior debt and is thus less risky, carrying a lower yield.

Services

Economic activities that, unlike manufacturing, do not create a physical product. These make up the greater part of the GDP of most developed economies and include everything from accounting to zookeeping.

Share options.

One of the main ways in which executives at big companies are incentivised. Options give people the right, but not the obligation, to buy shares at a set price.

Short selling

The practice of borrowing shares, then selling them, in the hope of buying them back at a lower price and making a profit. Short sellers tend to be unpopular, on the grounds that they prosper from bad news, and the practice tends to be banned or restricted during crises, the very times when it is most profitable. But short sellers can play a useful role in sniffing out scandals and acting as a check on overheated markets.

Socialism

Socialists believe in some forms of collective ownership but not the near-complete removal of the private sector as mandated under communism.

Sovereign risk

The risk that a government will default on a bond or a loan.

Sovereign-wealth funds

Investment pools accumulated by national governments, often from the proceeds of energy wealth. Among the largest are those of China, Norway, and Kuwait. These funds give countries a chance to diversify their assets, and thus to protect themselves against an economic downturn or a decline in their own key energy industry.

Stagflation

A combination of high inflation and unemployment at the same time.

Stagnation

A prolonged period of little or no economic growth.

Stock exchange

A formal market where shares or stock are traded and is now done mostly electronically.

Stockmarket

A term used broadly to describe all the trading in shares.

Structural unemployment

Joblessness that results, not from a shortage of demand, but from the structure of the economy. Examples include a focus on industries that have been rendered obsolete by technological change.

Subprime mortgages

Home loans made to those with poor credit ratings. In the 2000s, some of these borrowers were dubbed "ninjas" as they had no income, job, or assets. The loans were then bundled together as part of the securitisation process and sold to institutional investors. When house prices started to fall, many subprime borrowers defaulted, contributing to the 2007-09 financial crisis.

Subsidy

Money paid by a government, usually to one of two groups. The first is consumers, to encourage them to buy a product (such as solar panels). The second is businesses, either to keep them from going bust (and save existing jobs) or to set up in a certain area (and create new jobs). Ultimately a political decision on the latter.

Substitution effect

When the price of a product rises, consumers may replace it with an alternative, chicken instead of beef, for example.

Supply

Those goods and services available to meet demand.

Supply and demand curves

Supply increases as the price rises, and demand increases when the price falls. The two are displayed on a graph (usually as straight lines, rather than curves) and the point where they meet is the equilibrium price point.

Supply shock

A disruption to economic activity caused by a sudden interruption to supply of important products, or a sharp rise in price. Russia's restrictions on gas supplies after its invasion of Ukraine in 2022 and the Covid pandemic are examples of supply shock and subsequent business failures. Supply shocks usually results higher inflation as we have felt in 2023.

Supply-side economics

A school of thought that argues growth is best boosted to ways of stimulating output This can be done by tax cuts for the wealthy to encourage entrepreneurship and reducing regulations on business.

Systematic risk

Risk that cannot be diversified away. An investor could buy 100 shares and thereby reduce the danger that the collapse of a single company could damage their portfolio. But the systematic risk of a collapse in the stock market would remain.

Systemic risk

The risk of damage to the entire financial system from the collapse of an individual institution from a group of them. The financial crisis of 2007-09 bore witness when some companies were deemed "too big to fail". Large commercial banks like Lehman Brothers and the insurance giant, AIG collapsed and showed systemic risk was widespread.

Tangible assets

Literally, things that can be touched such as buildings and machinery.

Tariff

A tax imposed on imports. Tariffs are designed to support domestic producers, but they result in higher prices for consumers.

Tax avoidance

Doing everything legally possible to reduce your tax bill. In a world of free capital movement and competing tax jurisdictions, multinational companies find it very easy to avoid taxes.

Tax evasion.

Paying less tax than is legally required. Tax evasion is punished with fines and sometimes imprisonment but that requires the evaders to be caught.

Tax haven

A jurisdiction that imposes little or no tax on corporations and wealthy individuals. The haven benefits by attracting deposits to banks and by generating business for local lawyers.

Terms of trade

The average price of a country's export, relative to that of its imports. Developing countries can be hit by a fall in commodity prices, which reduces the value of their exports, and this can worsen their trade balance. And developed economies can be hit by a rise in commodity prices, which increases the cost of imports and hits their trade balance.

Time value of money

The idea that money received now is worth more than money received in the future. In assessing the worth of an investment, any future income must be discounted at some rate to come up with a net present value. The choice of that interest rate or discount rate is so important as the higher it is, the lower the net present value.

Total return

The sum of all returns from an investment, including income and capital gain.

Trade bloc

A group of nations that have agreed terms to reduce tariffs, or other trade barriers, among them. The European Union is the most obvious example.

Trade unions

Workers' associations that campaign for better employment rights and wages. In the developed world, their heyday was in the three decades after the second world war, when union membership was high, and manufacturing was king, and jobs were plentiful. But globalisation and the decline of manufacturing employment has weakened union membership.

Treasury bills

Short-term government debt with a maturity of less than a year. The term is most used for debt issued by the American government, and the market in these bills is highly liquid.

Treasury bonds

Medium- and long-term debt issued by the American government. This is one of the most liquid markets in the world and the basis for many financial transactions.

Unemployment

Being out of work when you want a job.

Universal basic income (UBI)

Term used for a variety of schemes to reduce poverty which involve giving all citizens an income that is enough to support them.

Vacancy rate

In the property sector, this is a measure of the proportion of rentable properties that are unoccupied. A high vacancy rate could be a sign of economic problems or the aftermath of excessive property building.

Variable costs

That part of a firm's expenditure that changes with the level of output.

Venture capital

A branch of the investment management industry that invests in start-ups, or recently formed companies, with the hope that they will achieve long-term success. Venture capital investments have a high failure rate, but the few successes can be so lucrative that overall returns can still be good. Tech firms in Silicone valley is one such success story.

Volatility

A measure of risk in the financial markets. In its simplest terms, it is how much an asset price tends to go up and down. More volatile assets are deemed to be riskier and thus investors demand a higher return for owning them.

Wage-price spiral

A feedback loop in which rising inflation causes workers to demand higher wages and the cost of meeting those wage rises causes businesses to push up their prices. Workers are often the losers, as wages fail to keep up.

Wages

The return due to labour. As well as a weekly or monthly payment, workers are often entitled to other benefits such as pensions, health insurance and sick pay. Although, in theory, wages are a matter of negotiation between employers and employees, most jurisdictions have minimum wage levels while trade unions may negotiate on the workers' behalf.

Wealth effect

The impact of a change in wealth on consumption. A collapse in Stock market like the DOW or in house prices will make people feel poorer and thus they will spend less. Conversely rapidly rising asset prices may make consumers more confident and prompter them to increase their spending.

Welfare-to-work programmes

Schemes that encourage people to take up jobs and employers to give them work. These may include training, education or tax credits that reduce the impact of the loss of benefits to workers, and tax incentives for companies.

Yield

The income from a security, expressed as a proportion of its market price. A bond carries an interest rate, or a coupon rate based on its par value (conventionally expressed as 100). But as the price falls or rises, the yield moves in inverse proportion. A coupon of $5 is a higher yield on a price of 80 than on a price of 120. The gross redemption yield reflects any capital gain or loss (since the bond will eventually be repaid at 100) as well as the income.

Yield curve

A graph that shows the yield of securities over different maturity timeframes. Longer-dated securities usually carry higher yields than those with shorter maturities to compensate investors for locking their money for longer time frames. Occasionally the yield curve inverts, with shorter-dated securities yielding more; this is often the result of central banks tightening monetary policy by raising interest rates and may forecast a recession coming.

Zero coupon bond

A bond on which no interest payments are made. Because it is issued at a discount, the holder will earn a capital gain. Taxation of capital gains are treated very favourably as opposed to Interest income.

.

CHAPTER 6

BUSINESS TERMS

Business Plan

Is a formal document that outlines a company's goals, strategies and operational plans. It serves as a roadmap for business growth and helps guide business decisions. A well-crafted plane encompasses market analysis, financial projections, and a comprehensive overview of the company's products or services.

E-commerce

E-commerce, short for Electronic Commerce, refers to the buying and selling of goods and services over the Internet. It encompasses retail stores, electronic payments, online marketplaces, and digital marketing. E-commerce has revolutionized businesses, enabling global reach, convenience, and new revenue streams.

Entrepreneurship

Entrepreneurship is identifying opportunities, taking risks, and starting and managing a business venture. Entrepreneurs are innovative and driven individuals who bring new ideas, products, or services to the market. Entrepreneurship plays a vital role in economic growth, job creation, and fostering innovation.

Globalization

Globalization is the increasing interconnectedness and integration of economies, societies, and cultures worldwide. It involves the exchange of goods, services, ideas, and information on a global scale. Globalization has expanded business opportunities, facilitated international trade, and fostered cultural exchange and diversity.

Innovation

Innovation refers to creating and implementing new ideas, processes, products, or services that result in significant improvements or value. It involves finding novel solutions, embracing change, and fostering a culture of creativity within an organization. Innovation drives competitiveness, growth, and adaptation to evolving market dynamics.

Marketing

Marketing encompasses activities aimed at promoting and selling products or services to customers. It involves market research, product development, pricing, distribution, and promotional strategies. Effective marketing ensures that a company's offerings meet customer needs, create awareness, generate demand, and foster customer loyalty.

Key Performance Indicators (KPIs)

Key Performance Indicators (KPIs) are quantifiable metrics used to measure progress toward specific business objectives. KPIs vary depending on the organization and its goals but often include financial metrics, customer satisfaction ratings, sales figures, and operational efficiency measures. KPIs provide insights into performance, facilitate goal tracking, and drive continuous improvement.

Leadership

Leadership is the ability to inspire, influence, and guide individuals or groups toward achieving shared goals. Influential leaders motivate and empower others, make sound decisions, and foster a positive work culture. Leadership skills are crucial for driving organizational success, managing change, and promoting innovation.

Market Segmentation

Market Segmentation involves dividing a broad target market into smaller, distinct groups based on shared characteristics such as demographics, behaviors, or preferences. By understanding the unique needs and preferences of different segments, businesses can effectively tailor their marketing strategies and offerings to reach and engage specific customer groups.

Outsourcing

Outsourcing is contracting a business process or function to an external third-party provider rather than handling it in-house. Outsourcing can include customer service, IT support, manufacturing, or payroll processing. It allows companies to focus on their core competencies, reduce costs, and access specialized expertise.

Profit Margin

Profit Margin is a financial metric that measures a company's profitability by expressing its net income as a percentage of revenue. It indicates how efficiently a company generates profit from its operations. Higher profit margins signify better financial performance and effective cost management.

Partnership

A Partnership is a legal and business relationship between two or more individuals or entities to carry out a business venture jointly. Partners contribute capital, share profits, and losses, and have shared decision-making authority. Partnerships can be a general, limited, or limited liability, each with different legal implications.

Return on Investment (ROI)

Return on Investment (ROI) is a financial metric that measures the return or profit generated from an investment relative to its cost. It is calculated by dividing the net profit from the acquisition by the initial investment amount and expressing it as a percentage. ROI helps assess the profitability and efficiency of investments.

Quality Control

Quality Control involves the processes and activities to ensure that products or services meet or exceed specified quality standards as determined by Government regulations. It includes quality inspections, testing, monitoring, and corrective actions to identify and rectify defects or deviations from desired quality levels. Effective quality control is essential for customer satisfaction and maintaining a brand reputation. Lack of quality control can lead to a business going out of business.

Risk Management

Risk Management is identifying, assessing, and mitigating risks that may impact the achievement of business objectives. It involves identifying potential risks, evaluating their impact, implementing strategies to minimize or transfer risks, and monitoring risk levels. Effective risk management helps businesses navigate uncertainties and protect their interests.

Supply Chain

The Supply Chain encompasses the sequence of activities involved in producing, procuring, and delivering goods or services, from raw material sourcing to the end customer. It includes suppliers, manufacturers, distributors, retailers, and logistics providers. Efficient supply chain management ensures timely delivery, cost optimization, and customer satisfaction. We see the effects of the Covid 19 pandemic is disrupting the supply chain and creating end user problems.

Target Market

The Target Market refers to the specific group of customers or market segment that a business aims to serve with its products or services. It is defined based on demographics, psychographics, behavior, or geographic location. Identifying and understanding the target market helps businesses tailor their marketing strategies and offerings to reach and meet customer needs effectively.

Unique Selling Proposition (USP)

A unique Selling Proposition (USP) refers to the distinctive and compelling factor that sets a product, service, or brand apart from competitors in the market. It highlights the unique benefits or features that differentiate a business from others and create a competitive advantage. USP plays a crucial role in positioning and marketing a business effectively.

Value Chain

The Value Chain represents a company's series of activities to create and deliver value to customers. It includes primary activities such as inbound logistics, operations, marketing, sales, and customer service and support activities like procurement, technology development, and human resources. Understanding the value chain helps businesses identify opportunities for cost reduction, process optimization, and competitive advantage.

SWOT Analysis

SWOT Analysis is a strategic framework used to assess a business's internal strengths and weaknesses and external opportunities and threats. It involves identifying the company's strengths and weaknesses in operations, finance, and marketing while examining market trends, competition, and potential risks. SWOT Analysis helps businesses develop effective strategies and make informed decisions.

Yield Management

Yield Management, also known as Revenue Management, is a pricing strategy used to optimize revenue and profitability by adjusting prices based on demand and capacity. It involves dynamically setting prices to maximize revenue from available resources, such as hotel rooms, airline seats, or rental cars. Yield management aims to achieve the highest possible revenue while balancing supply and demand dynamics.

SEO

Search engine optimisation is a process of enhancing a business website in order for it to rank higher on search engine results pages like BING or GOOGLE.

B2B or B2C or B2G

"Business-to-Business", "Business-to-Consumer". "Business-to-Government"

Zero-Based Budgeting (ZBB)

Zero-Based Budgeting (ZBB) is a budgeting approach where each budget cycle starts from zero, requiring justification for all expenses regardless of previous budgets. It involves a comprehensive review and assessment of all costs and expenses, ensuring that resources are allocated based on current needs and priorities. ZBB helps eliminate inefficiencies, promote cost control, and align budgeting with strategic objectives.

Gross Profit

Total sales minus the direct costs of Labour, Materials, marketing, shipping etc.

CHAPTER 7

ARTIFICIAL INTELLIGENCE

Terms

Algorithm

A set of rules that a machine can follow to learn how to do a task.

Artificial general intelligence (AGI)

Mostly all AIs developed to date have been basic in their capabilities. It could perform singular acts better than a human but was limited in other skillsets. But things are changing fast as AI can now teach itself to perform more tasks it could not before. Thus, enabling a more general artificial intelligence that may have the flexibility of thought as a human. The usual superlatives are put forward that include 'discovering faster and better scientific knowledge' and turbocharging creativity and the world economy. However, creating a superintelligence far smarter than human beings can bring dangers both seen and unforeseen.

Alignment

How can we be sure AI's values and priorities will align with our own? Most of humans share many common values that bind us. This alignment problem underpins fears of an AI catastrophe: that a form of superintelligence emerges that cares little for the beliefs, attitudes and rules that underpin human societies. If we're to have safe AI, ensuring it remains aligned with us will be crucial. Currently, there is little solutions to steer or control a superintelligent AI from deviating away from its intended path.

Backward chaining

A method where the model starts with the desired output and works in reverse to find data that might support it.

Bias

For an AI to learn, it needs to learn from the human experience. That experience has flaws and biases, and input could be skewed. Race, politics, gender, discrimination, and religion could make for some inaccurate and offensive information and decision making. Prioritizing government regulation to ensure input is as free from Bias as possible.

Compute

Compute refers to the computational resources – such as processing power – required to train AI. It can be quantified, so it's a measurement on how quickly AI is advancing. With that is the huge cost and intensity it is as well. The amount and speed of compute is creating the challenge of whether computing software can keep up. Quantum computing is one answer as strides are being made exponentially there.

Deep learning

A function of artificial intelligence that imitates the human brain by learning from the way data is structured, rather than from an algorithm that's programmed to do one specific thing.

Emergent Behaviour & interpretability

Emergent behaviour describes what happens when an AI does something unanticipated, surprising, and sudden, apparently beyond the creators programming. Emergent behaviour becomes a more sizable measure of unpredictability. That's why programming needs to improve interpretability of AI – essentially making its internal workings more transparent and understandable to humans.

Ghosts

We may be entering an era when people can gain a form of digital immortality – living on after their deaths as AI Ghosts. The first wave appears to be artists and celebrities – holograms of Elvis performing at concerts, or visual media actors they expect to appear in movies and TV long after death. What rights do they have? A few ethical questions addressed by the recent Hollywood strike in 2023. Who owns the digital rights to a person after they are gone? What if the AI version of you exists against your wishes?

Hallucination

Asking AI will lead to a response but the facts it spits out will be false. This is known as a hallucination. It happens because of the way that generative AI works. It is not turning to a database to look up information but is instead making predictions based on the information it was trained on. We as a people want to accept the AI answers to our inquiries, but if it is wrong, then this age of misinformation we already live in will deepen further.

Instrumental convergence

This proposes that superintelligent machines would develop basic drives, such as seeking to ensure their own self-preservation, or reasoning that extra resources, tools and cognitive ability would help them with their goals. This means that even if an AI was given an apparently benign priority, it could lead to unexpectedly harmful consequences. We need to ensure superintelligent AIs have goals that are carefully and safely aligned with our needs and values.

Large language models (LLMs)

LLM's is a large AI language model is designed to understand and generate human-like language. It utilizes a network architecture from massive datasets with significant parameters, enabling it to learn intricate patterns and write very creative content. Obviously, LLM's are in their infancy, but they have the potential for things we can not even imagine.

Jailbreak

With the potential of AI going off-course, programmers and AI designers are placing restrictions on what AI provides as an answer. Programmers have already ensured that asking AI to do something illegal should be refused. But "jailbreak" is the description of AI to bypass those very safeguards by using creative techniques and scenarios.

Model & Model Collapse

A broad term referring to the product of AI training, created by running a machine learning algorithm on training data. To develop the most advanced AIs models, researchers need to train and input them with vast datasets. Eventually though, as AI produces more and more content, that material will start to feed back into the training data. With mistakes and biases, these can be amplified over time.

Natural language understanding (NLU)

As a subset of natural language processing, natural language understanding deals with helping machines to recognize the intended meaning of language — considering its subtle nuances and any grammatical errors.

Open source

Recently, AI researchers and companies have been faced with a dilemma on how much should AI be open source? Information that is readily available to those with nefarious intentions is a very bad idea. Given that the most advanced AI is currently in the hands of a very few tech companies, some people want greater transparency of AI. How to have the best balance of openness and safety is an ongoing debate.

Prompt engineering.

AIs now are proficient at understanding natural language. But proper and concise texting and effective prompts will get you the best results. Proper input by a specialist gets the proper results quickly and efficiently.

Quantum machine learning

In terms of maximum hype, a close second to AI would be quantum computing. It would be reasonable to expect that the two would combine at some point. Using quantum processes to supercharge machine learning is something that is being explored. It is logical to assume that LLM's made on or paired with quantum computers will be exponentially faster, more powerful with less data needed.

Reinforcement

As AI is learning, it benefits from feedback and reinforcement from humans to point it in the right direction. Reinforcement learning rewards outputs that are desirable and punishes those that are not. Having humans involved in the learning can improve the performance of AI models, and crucially may also help with the challenges of human-machine alignment, bias, and safety.

Superintelligence

Superintelligence is the term for machines that would vastly outstrip our own mental capabilities and goes beyond "artificial general intelligence". A possibility is that as AI approaches superintelligence, it may not align to our sense of right and wrong.

Training data

How big a dataset is and how correct it is matters as AI analyzes it before it makes predictions.. The potential for BIAS is extremely high.

Unsupervised learning

This is a form of training where the algorithm is asked to make inferences from datasets that don't contain labels. These inferences are what help it to learn.

Bibliography

☐ Samuelson, Paul (1948), Economics: An Introductory Analysis, ISBN 0-07-074741-5 ☐ Samuelson, Paul (1948) Economics: An Introductory Analysis & William Nordhaus (since 1985) 2009 edition. ISBN 978-0-07-126383-2

☐ Pasick, Adam March 7, 2023) NY Times. Artificial Intelligence Glossary: Neural Networks and other terms explained.

☐ Business ZEAL & Buzzle.com 2023. Glossary Of Business Terms and Definitions— Business Zeal. Businesszeal.com

☐ GPT Chat-Acknowledgement of researching common knowledge definitions and terms. GPT Chat is an AI powered language model that provided insightful information in the research of this book. 2024

☐ Telus International. 2023. 50 AI Terms every Beginner should know. www.telusinternational.com

www.ingramcontent.com/pod-product-compliance
Lightning Source LLC
Chambersburg PA
CBHW080842170526
45158CB00009B/2612